Quality Inspection Checklists

RYAN BRAUTOVICH

Copyright © 2012 Ryan Brautovich

All rights reserved. No part of this book may be reproduced or transmitted in any form or by any means, electronic or mechanical, including photocopying, recording, or by any information storage and retrieval system, without the written permission of the Publisher.

Printed in the United States of America

October 2012

ISBN: 978-0-9864404-2-7

"Quality is never an accident; it is always the result of high intention, sincere effort, intelligent direction and skillful execution; it represents the wise choice of many alternatives."

~ William A. Foster

The Construction H.E.L.P. Foundation's Home Construction Audit program makes it easy and painless – through the use of our Home Building System – to understand how to build a home, how to manage your contractor, and how to protect yourself from being taken advantage of and scammed. We demystify the process and remove all of the contractor jargon to give you the building process in easy-to-understand, plain English. The Construction H.E.L.P. Foundation's founder and building expert Ryan Brautovich's exclusive 4-step home building system will ensure you are on the right track – and on budget – every step of the way. For more information about the Construction H.E.L.P Foundation, the Home Construction Audit Program, or any of the educational products, homeowner services, or construction seminars available in your area, please visit **www.HomeConstructionAudit.com**, or **www.ConHelp4U.org**

TABLE OF CONTENTS

BLOCK FOUNDATIONS	1
BRICK/ROCK LABOR	3
CABINETS	4
CLEANING (FINAL)	6
CLEANING (ROUGH)	8
CLEARING AND GRADING (GRADING 1)	9
CLEARING AND GRADING (GRADING 2)	10
CLEARING AND GRADING (GRADING 3)	11
COUNTER TOPS	12
DECK AND PORCH LABOR	13
DRIVES AND WALKWAYS	14
DRYWALL	15
ELECTRIC (FINAL)	17
ELECTRIC (ROUGH)	18
FIREPLACES (FINAL)	20
FIREPLACES (ROUGH)	21
FLOOR COVERING (CARPET)	22
FLOOR COVERINGS	24
FOOTINGS	26
FRAMING LABOR	27
GARAGE DOORS	31
GUTTERING	32
HEATING AND AIR CONDITIONING (FINAL)	33
HEATING AND AIR CONDITIONING (ROUGH)	35

INSULATION	37
LANDSCAPING	40
MIRRORS	42
PAINTING (FINAL)	44
PAINTING (ROUGH)	46
PAINTING (TOUCH-UP)	48
PLUMBING (FINAL)	49
PLUMBING (ROUGH)	52
PLUMBING (UNDERGROUND)	53
POURED WALL FOUNDATIONS	54
ROOFING LABOR	56
SHELVING	57
SHOWER DOORS	58
SHUTTERS	59
SIDING AND CORNICE LABOR	60
SLABS	61
STAIRS (PREBUILT)	63
TRIM LABOR	64
TRIM LABOR (LOCK-OUT)	66
WATERPROOFING	67
WINDOW AND DOOR INSTALLATION	68

QUALITY INSPECTION CHECKLIST

BLOCK FOUNDATIONS

Pre-Work Inspection: (to be completed prior to beginning work)
Date Completed _____

___ Contractor has picked up and signed for plans.

___ Work area is clean and free of debris.

___ Footing(s) are poured. Alignment and square corners have been verified.

___ Dimensions are correct.

___ Stakes are set and locations are correct.

___ Straightness (alignment) of lines is verified.

___ All setbacks, bay windows, fireplace(s), porches, stoops, etc., are clearly marked and dimensions checked.

___ All materials are on site and ready to be used.

Final Inspection: (to be completed before Trade Contractor leaves jobsite)   Date Completed _____

___ Verify all walls are true, plumb, and square.

___ There are no cracks in excess of 1/4 inch in width or displacement.

___ The variance does not exceed 1/2 inch out of level in 20 feet, with no ridges or depressions in excess of 1/4 inch within any 32-inch measurement.

___ Foundation walls are not more than 1 inch out of level over the entire surface and do not vary more than 1/2 inch out of square when measured along the diagonal of a 6x8x10-foot triangle at any corner.

___ Header block are used for all slab areas.

___ Cap block are used for all garage and drive-under walls.

___ Every third cell is filled in all areas of the foundation that are more than 36 inches in height.

___ All lines and pinholes are filled.

___ All excess mortar between blocks has been removed.

___ Stucco finish is smooth and a minimum of 3/8 inch of Portland cement parging is applied from footing(s) to finish grade.

___ Anchor bolts are 6 feet on center and not more than 12 inches from corners.

___ The trench(es) at foundation/footings is free and clear of all material and debris.

___ All excess material is stacked and protected from weather.

___ Jobsite area is clean and all excess (runoff) concrete has been removed to driveway.

___ Footing batterboards have been removed and stacked with excess material.

___ The field count of blocks has been done.

___ Field measurement of stucco is applied.

___ Field count of unused materials has been done.

QUALITY INSPECTION CHECKLIST

BRICK/ROCK LABOR

Pre-Work Inspection: (to be completed prior to beginning work)
Date Completed _____

___ Plans have been reviewed with Contractor.
___ House is ready for brick.
___ Brick lintels are installed correctly, are level and of proper length.
___ Insulation board is installed in all areas with no open areas and no broken or damaged boards.
___ Material at jobsite is ready to be used.
___ Site is clean and free of debris.
___ Windows are intact with none broken.
___ OSHA-approved scaffolding, rigging, and safety equipment is in use.

Final Inspection: (to be completed before Trade Contractor leaves jobsite)   Date Completed _____

___ Windows are intact with none broken.
___ Brick/Rock is level, plumb, and square.
___ Decorative accents are per plan.
___ Brick/Rock is completely clean with no mortar drips, smears, or runs.
___ Jobsite is clean and all debris moved to designated area.
___ Excess bricks/rocks and mortar are stacked on pallets. Mortar is covered in plastic.
___ Excess material is counted.
___ Field measurements have been made of actual bricks used.
___ All scaffolding and walkboards are removed with no damage to brick.

QUALITY INSPECTION CHECKLIST

CABINETS

Pre-Work Inspection: (to be completed prior to beginning work)
Date Completed _____

- ___ Color selection sheet(s) has been received by Contractor.
- ___ Cabinet areas are field-measured (after drywall has been installed).
- ___ Windows are intact with none broken.
- ___ Tubs are covered and undamaged.
- ___ Temporary stairs (if required), temporary handrails, and safety bracing are installed.
- ___ House is broom-swept, clean, and free of debris

Final Inspection: (to be completed before Trade Contractor leaves jobsite)   Date Completed _____

- ___ Windows are intact with none broken.
- ___ Temporary handrails, safety bracing, etc., are intact.
- ___ Cabinets are installed per plan (correct number, size, etc.).
- ___ Cabinets are level and plumb.
- ___ Cabinets are secured correctly and tightly to wall.
- ___ Color of cabinets and countertops is correct.
- ___ Colored caulk is used if colored cabinets and countertops.
- ___ Cabinet doors and drawer fronts are level and square.
- ___ Cabinet faces and corners are level and plumb.
- ___ All doors and drawers open and close correctly.
- ___ Correct hardware is installed—square, plumb, and correctly.
- ___ Screws attaching hardware have not splintered wood.
- ___ Kick plates are installed with no gaps or holes.
- ___ HVAC vent is cut correctly (if required). Shoe molding will fit below vent.
- ___ Cabinets are undamaged.
- ___ Cabinets are intact with no unfilled holes.

___ Shelves are level and undamaged.
___ The number of shelves is correct.
___ For adjustable shelves, all holders fit, none are missing, and are level.
___ For all rollout shelves, operation is smooth and shelves track tight and secure.
___ Lazy susan(s) are installed plumb, work correctly, and are secured tightly.
___ Cabinets are clean inside and out.
___ Countertops are protected with cardboard that is taped securely.
___ House is clean, broom-swept, and debris removed.

QUALITY INSPECTION CHECKLIST

CLEANING (FINAL)

Pre-Work Inspection: (to be completed prior to beginning work)
Date Completed _____

___ Verified any special items with Contractor.

___ House is clean with no trash or debris.

___ Faceplates are in place on all switches and receptacles.

___ Cabinets are complete with hardware, shelves, etc.

___ Appliances are installed.

___ Drywall and painting are complete.

___ All trim is installed.

___ All flooring is installed.

___ Doors and hardware are installed.

Final Inspection: (to be completed before Trade Contractor leaves jobsite)   Date Completed _____   NOTE: All areas that are to be "dusted" free of dust or grit when a hand is brushed across the surface.

___ All walls, baseboards, chair rails, ets. are dusted with no smudge marks.

___ Vinyl, wood, tile flooring is mopped and cleaned with no black marks or adhesive.

___ All window sills and trim are dusted with no smudges.

___ Handrails, stair treads, and pickets are clean and free of smudges, dirt, and dust.

___ Mirrors are clean and shiny with no drywall dust on tops or sides.

___ Sinks, showers, tubs, and toilets are clean and shiny with no drywall dust on top ledges.

___ Faucets, showerheads, and other such fixtures are clean and shiny.

___ Ductwork and return-air grills are vacuumed.

___ Windows are clean and shiny, including frames.

___ All hardware is clean and shiny (towel bars, toilet paper holders, etc.).

___ Cabinets are clean inside and out with no drywall dust on tops of cabinets.

___ Countertops are clean and shiny.

___ Appliances are clean inside and out.

___ Light fixtures are clean and shiny with no fingerprints, dust, or smudges.

___ Shelving is dusted and clean.

___ Carpet is vacuumed with no spots.

___ Garage, storage rooms, and unfinished basement are clean and broom-swept.

___ Thresholds are clean, free of dirt, mud, etc.

___ Fireplace fronts and mantels are clean and free of dust and dirt.

___ Ceiling fans are dusted or damp-wiped and clean, free of dust, smudges, etc.

___ Tubs and shower covers are removed.

___ Trash is removed and house is in "move-in" condition.

QUALITY INSPECTION CHECKLIST

CLEANING (ROUGH)

Pre-Work Inspection: (to be completed prior to beginning work)
Date Completed _____

___ House has been reviewed with Contractor for any special instructions.
___ House is clean with no trash or debris.
___ Tubs, sinks, countertops, stair treads, hardwood, vinyl, etc., are all covered and protected.
___ Faceplates are in place on all switches and receptacles.
___ Cabinets are complete (hardware, shelves, etc.).
___ Appliances are installed.
___ Drywall and painting are complete.
___ All trim is installed.
___ Vinyl, wood, and tile flooring is installed and protected.
___ Doors are installed.
___ All hardware is installed.

Final Inspection: (to be completed before Trade Contractor leaves jobsite)   Date Completed _____

___ Floors are broom-swept and clean.
___ Windows are clean inside and out (Windows are not scratched).
___ Window frames are clean inside and out.
___ Cabinets (drawers, tops, and front) are cleaned inside and out.
___ Trim is dusted.
___ House is ready for carpet and final punch-out.
___ Protection for all tubs, floors, etc., is still in place.

QUALITY INSPECTION CHECKLIST

CLEARING AND GRADING (GRADING 1)

Pre-Work Inspection: (to be completed prior to beginning work)
Date Completed _____

___ House corners are staked and lot pins are in place.
___ Area to be cleared is clearly marked and the Contractor and Trade Contractor have walked the area together.
___ Any natural undisturbed area is marked and understood.
___ Direction of water drainage has been determined and is understood.
___ Area to place trees, stumps, and development debris has been designated by the Contractor and the Trade Contractor understands the location and how the debris is to be collected, etc.

Final Inspection: (to be completed before Trade Contractor leaves jobsite)   Date Completed _____

___ All debris has been removed from the lot.
___ Lot is roughly level with no holes, hills, valleys, etc.
___ Pad has been cut and measured to determine correctness of size.
___ House pad is correctly located.
___ Driveway is cut and ready for base material.
___ Undisturbed natural area is still undisturbed.

QUALITY INSPECTION CHECKLIST

CLEARING AND GRADING (GRADING 2)

Pre-Work Inspection: (to be completed prior to beginning work)
Date Completed _____

___ Lot is clear of any construction debris.
___ Foundation is complete.
___ Rough mechanicals are installed in slab area.

Final Inspection: (to be completed before Trade Contractor leaves jobsite)   Date Completed _____

___ Slab is backfilled. All rough mechanicals are intact and undamaged.
___ All foundation drains are clear of dirt and extend 6 inches above top of footings, as required.
___ Front- and backyard are graded.
___ Swales and berms are established.
___ Water flow direction is correct.
___ All excess dirt has been removed.
___ Lot is clear and free of building debris.

QUALITY INSPECTION CHECKLIST

CLEARING AND GRADING (GRADING 3)

Pre-Work Inspection: (to be completed prior to beginning work)
Date Completed _____

___ Lot is clear and free of construction debris.

___ Any repairs required for swales and berms are understood.

Final Inspection: (to be completed before Trade Contractor leaves jobsite)   Date Completed _____

___ Swales and berms are correct. Water direction is correct.

___ Final grading of the lot is complete. Lot is ready for landscaping,

___ Eight (8) inches of foundation clear around entire house.

___ Foundation drains are visible and clear, as required.

QUALITY INSPECTION CHECKLIST

COUNTER TOPS

Pre-Work Inspection: (to be completed prior to beginning work)

Date Completed _____

___ Color, and material selection sheet has been given to Contractor.

___ Cabinet areas have been field-measured.

___ Windows are intact with none broken.

___ Tubs are covered and undamaged.

___ Temporary stairs, if required, temporary handrails, and safety bracing are installed.

___ House is broom-swept, clean, and free of debris.

Final Inspection: (to be completed before Trade Contractor leaves jobsite)   Date Completed _____

___ Windows are intact with none broken.

___ Temporary handrails, safety bracing, etc., are intact.

___ Counter tops are installed per plan (correct number, size, material, color, etc.).

___ Tops are level and plumb.

___ Tops are secured correctly and tightly to wall.

___ Color(s) of counter tops are correct.

___ Counter tops are undamaged.

___ Counter tops are protected with cardboard and taped securely.

___ House is clean, broom-swept, and debris has been removed.

QUALITY INSPECTION CHECKLIST

DECK AND PORCH LABOR

Initial Inspection: (to be completed prior to beginning work)
Date Completed _____

___ Deck and/or porch plans are correct.
___ Site is clean and free of debris.
___ House is sided and ready for deck/porch.
___ Material is on site and ready to be used.
___ Windows are intact with none broken.
___ Electricity is available.

Final Inspection: (to be completed before Trade Contractor leaves jobsite)   Date Completed _____

___ Deck/porch is built per plan.
___ Deck/porch is level.
___ Decking is 5/4-board bullnosed. Spacing is correct.
___ Deck/porch is firmly bolted to house with no give or sway.
___ Deck posts are 4x4 (unless otherwise noted on plan) and installed plumb.
___ Post bases are shackle-bolted and set in concrete.
___ All corners of all handrails terminate with a 4x4 deck post.
___ Handrails are secure with no give, sway, or movement.
___ Pickets are secure and correctly nailed.
___ Step run and rise are correct.
___ Landings are per plan if required.
___ Jobsite is clean. Construction debris and trash have been removed to correct area.
___ Excess material is stacked in garage, field counted, and noted on purchase order.

QUALITY INSPECTION CHECKLIST

DRIVES and WALKWAYS

Pre-Work Inspection: (to be completed prior to beginning work)
Date Completed _____

___ Plans have been reviewed with Contractor.

___ Work area is clean and free of debris.

___ Drive and walks are staked.

___ Dimensions are correct.

___ All materials are on site and ready to be used.

___ Clear access and a stable base is in place for concrete trucks.

___ Landscape irrigation sleeves have been installed.

Final Inspection: (to be completed before Trade Contractor leaves jobsite)   Date Completed _____

___ Drive connection to garage is such that no water may enter garage.

___ Drive, walkways, and patio/porch have been checked to ensure proper water runoff.

___ No aggregate is exposed.

___ No cracks or displacements are visible.

___ Expansion joints are installed properly.

___ Dimensions are correct.

___ Surface is broom-finished.

___ Any concrete runoff has been removed.

___ Jobsite is clean and free of debris.

___ Drive barricade board is installed. No vehicles, equipment, materials, trash, concrete spoils, etc, should EVER be on finished drive!

QUALITY INSPECTION CHECKLIST

DRYWALL

Initial Inspection: (to be completed prior to beginning work)
Date Completed _____

___ House is clean and free of debris.
___ Material is stocked and ready to be used. Second floor should be supported under any area where drywall is stacked.
___ Windows are intact—none broken.
___ Temporary stairs, temporary handrails, and safety bracing are in place.
___ Tubs and showers are covered and protected.
___ HVAC Ducts are installed and registers are square.
___ Electrical is installed and all boxes are plumb, level, and square.
___ Can lighting is installed and centered as needed. Cans are locked in place (so they won't be knocked out of alignment by the drywallers).
___ Plumbing is installed and properly supported to eliminate wall noise.
___ Framing items are correct—no bowed studs, no nails protruding into drywall area. All house details are framed (access holes, stairways, special ceilings, scuttle holes, etc.).
___ Fireplace is set and is level and plumb.

Final Inspection: (to be completed before Trade Contractor leaves jobsite)   Date Completed _____

___ Drywall is tightly fitted to walls.
___ Drywall does not float in any area, and is secure at all openings (closets, windows, doors, fireplace, etc.).
___ Nails and screws are 16 inches on center.
___ All fasteners are mudded, taped, and sanded.
___ Joints are smooth and sanded.
___ There are no gaps, spaces, or broken pieces of drywall at electrical boxes.
___ Electrical boxes are free of mud and debris.

___ There are no gaps larger than 1/4 inch around tubs, showers, fireboxes, windows, and doors.

___ There are no hairline cracks in any corner, vault, tray, or ceiling line.

___ There are no un-drywalled holes left in storage rooms, garages, etc.

___ **All** drywall joints are taped, mudded, and sanded, including storage rooms, etc.

___ Paper is smooth, not over-sanded.

___ Walls are flat and smooth, with no visible bumps in joints due to rough edges.

___ Ceiling Lines are straight and crisp (including center line of vault).

___ All corners are taped and smooth with corner bead/bullnose.

___ Temporary handrails and bracing are intact.

___ There are no broken windows.

___ Tubs and showers are covered and undamaged.

___ Drywall mud has been removed from floor. Floor is broom-swept. All debris has been removed.

QUALITY INSPECTION CHECKLIST

ELECTRIC (FINAL)

Pre-Work Inspection: (to be completed prior to beginning work)
Date Completed _____

___ House is clean and free of debris.

___ Tubs, sinks, etc., are covered and protected, and free of damage.

___ Drywall is complete with no damage.

___ Painting is complete with no damage.

___ All receptacle boxes are clean and free of drywall mud and other debris.

___ House is at stage for final electrical to be completed.

___ House is broom-swept, clean, and free of debris.

Final Inspection: (to be completed before Trade Contractor leaves jobsite)   Date Completed _____

___ All faceplates are installed square, plumb, and snug against walls.

___ All receptacles are tested and all work as required.

___ All appliances are hooked up and tested.

___ Garbage disposal is tested.

___ All light fixtures are installed and tested.

___ Smoke detectors are hooked up and tested.

___ HVAC units are hooked up and tested.

___ Bath fans and ceiling fans are hooked up and tested.

___ Doorbell is hooked up and tested.

___ Outdoor boxes must be weatherproofed.

___ House and Site are clean and free of debris.

QUALITY INSPECTION CHECKLIST

ELECTRIC (ROUGH)

Pre-Work Inspection: (to be completed prior to beginning work)
Date Completed _____

- ___ Contractor has Electrical plans.
- ___ Tubs and showers are covered and protected, and are free of damage.
- ___ Temporary handrails and safety bracing is in place as needed.
- ___ If house requires two HVAC units, the attic access is ready and units are installed for wiring.
- ___ House is roofed and shingled.
- ___ House is broom-swept, clean, and free of debris.

Final Inspection: (to be completed before Trade Contractor leaves jobsite)   Date Completed _____

- ___ Temporary power pole is set and temporary power is on.
- ___ Wiring is complete for light switches and receptacles per plan.
- ___ All receptacle boxes are set square, plumb, and 3/8 inch past stud.
- ___ Bracing for ceiling fans, as required, is installed.
- ___ Wiring for thermostats is complete.
- ___ Wiring for smoke detectors, washer, dryer, flood lights, holiday lighting, etc., is complete.
- ___ Wiring for HVAC units is complete.
- ___ Wiring is sized correctly for units being installed.
- ___ Wiring for outside receptacles is complete.
- ___ Wiring for low voltage, cable, telephone, speaker wire, etc. is complete.
- ___ Outside disconnects are installed.
- ___ Metal boxes must be grounded (jumper/pig tail from ground wire to green screw)
- ___ Breaker box is installed.
- ___ Breakers are clearly and legibly labeled.

___ Water and gas line are bonded, as required.

___ Emergency stickers are in place on breaker box.

___ Inspection has been passed.

___ Site and house is clean and free of debris.

QUALITY INSPECTION CHECKLIST

FIREPLACES (FINAL)

Pre-Work Inspection: (to be completed prior to beginning work)
Date Completed _____

___ Room(s) in which fireplace(s) is to be installed are clean and free of debris.

___ Fireplace is level.

___ Drywall is complete.

Final Inspection: (to be completed before Trade Contractor leaves jobsite)   Date Completed _____

___ Fireplace is still level, plumb, and square.

___ Screen is in place.

___ Flue opens and closes correctly.

___ Fresh air vent works.

___ Face installed correctly—level, plumb, and square.

___ Gap around the face is no more than 1/8 inch.

___ Mantle is level, square, and snug with no more than 1/8 inch caulked.

___ Hearth is installed level, square, and plumb/flat floor—flush with floor.

___ Penetration at gas line (through fireplace wall) is completely caulked and sealed with fireproof caulking.

___ Gas starter is installed.

___ Gas starter checked and working.

___ Glass fireplace doors are installed level, plumb, and square.

___ Cap or shroud is installed on chimney.

___ House is clean and free of debris.

QUALITY INSPECTION CHECKLIST

FIREPLACES (ROUGH)

Pre-Work Inspection: (to be completed prior to beginning work)
Date Completed ____

___ Correct fireplace is onsite to be installed.

___ Room(s) in which fireplace is to be installed are clean and free of debris.

___ Framing is complete.

___ There are no cuts in the subfloor.

Rough Inspection: (to be completed before Trade Contractor leaves jobsite)   Date Completed ____

___ Fireplace is installed level, plumb, and square.

___ Fireplace does not extend more than 3/8 inch on any side.

___ There are no cuts in the subfloor.

___ Trash is removed from the house to dumpster or designated area.

___ Gas line penetration is "draftstopped".

___ Fireplace is installed as directed by the manufacturer.

___ Vents are installed per manufacturer's specifications.

QUALITY INSPECTION CHECKLIST

FLOOR COVERING (CARPET)

Initial Inspection (prior to installing carpet): (to be completed prior to beginning work)   Date Completed _____

- ___ House is clean and free of debris.
- ___ Drive is barricaded (Carpet layers can layout and cut carpet on drive. They do not park on drive.)
- ___ House has been rough cleaned.
- ___ Windows have been cleaned.
- ___ Floors are clean and ready to be prepped.
- ___ Hardwood and vinyl flooring is clean and undamaged.
- ___ Drywall is complete.
- ___ Painting is complete.
- ___ Cabinets, toilets, etc., are all installed.
- ___ Light fixtures are installed.
- ___ Switch and receptacle covers are in place.
- ___ All hardware is installed.
- ___ Garage is clean, broom-swept, and ready to be used to cut carpet.
- ___ Slab and Sub-floor and been grinded level.

Final Inspection (after installing carpet): (to be completed before Trade Contractor leaves jobsite)   Date Completed _____

- ___ Floor is level with no underlying lumps, bumps, hilly areas, depressions, etc.
- ___ Carpet is cut to within 1/8 inch of wall.
- ___ Transition strips are installed between vinyl and carpet and firmly seated.
- ___ Pad and carpet are firmly attached to tack strip.
- ___ Carpet is butted firmly against tile and hardwood flooring.

___ No gaps are visible.

___ Seams are very inconspicuous.

___ Carpet is well stretched so that it is tight and has no wrinkles.

___ No obvious color variations are visible.

___ Carpet has been inspected under normal interior lighting and also in sunlight from windows.

___ Left-over carpet is in garage, store room, or laundry area.

___ House is clean and free of debris.

___ Jobsite is clean.

QUALITY INSPECTION CHECKLIST

FLOOR COVERINGS

Initial Inspection (prior to installing parquet, hardwood, or vinyl flooring): (to be completed prior to beginning work)

Date Completed _____

___ Color selection has been verified.
___ Jobsite is clean and free of debris.
___ House is clean and broom-swept.
___ Driveway is clean and barricaded.
___ Temporary handrails, bracing, etc., are in place.
___ Floor is level with no more than 1/4 inch in 32-inches deviation.
___ Floor is clean.
___ Subflooring cracks are filled and sanded level.
___ No bumps, overlaps, etc., are in subfloor or slab.
___ Subflooring or slab is dry.

Final Inspection (after installing parquet, hardwood, or vinyl flooring): (to be completed before Trade Contractor leaves jobsite)

Date Completed _____

___ Floors are level after installation of floor covering with no deviation more than 1/4 inch in 32 inches.
___ Floor coverings are cut within 1/8 inch of wall.
___ Floor coverings are firmly attached with no bubbles, nail pops, lumps, bumps, etc.
___ Pattern of vinyl is laid square, and correct, and in a manner that helps diminish any wall deflections.
___ Floor coverings are correct at door casings. Subflooring or slab is not visible.
___ Floor coverings are correct at toilets.
___ Vinyl is flush with cabinets and tubs.

___ Floor coverings are correct at all ducts.

___ Hardwood flooring does not have gaps, splinters, or loose areas.

___ Tile, hardwood, and vinyl flooring has been inspected under normal interior lighting and also in sunlight from windows. No defects were found.

___ Floor coverings are protected from damage.

___ House is clean with all working areas broom-swept.

___ Debris and trash have been removed to designated trash site.

___ Left-over vinyl, tile, tile grout, and hardwood flooring has been stacked in the garage, store room, or laundry area.

QUALITY INSPECTION CHECKLIST

FOOTINGS

Pre-Work Inspection: (to be completed prior to beginning work)
Date Completed _____

___ Contractor has building plans.

___ Work area is clean and free of debris.

___ Site is cleared and pad cut.

___ House is laid out, stakes set, and dimensions match plans.

___ House fits on lot within building and easement lines.

___ Straightness (alignment) of lines has been verified.

___ All setbacks, bay windows, fireplaces, porches, stoops, etc., are clearly marked and dimensions checked.

___ Utility sleeves, and UFER ground are in place.

___ Area is cleared and ready for cement truck access.

___ Driveway is cut and filled with stone.

Final Inspection: (to be completed before Trade Contractor leaves jobsite)   Date Completed _____

___ Depth and width of concrete is correct.

___ Corners are square.

___ Footings are level and plumb.

___ Footings are straight with no more than a 4-inch deviation in 20 feet.

___ All setback and foundation dimensions have been verified.

___ Overall dimensions have been verified against plans.

___ No aggregate is exposed in any area.

___ Site is clean and free of excess concrete.

___ Concrete Batch tickets have been collected from concrete truck drivers.

QUALITY INSPECTION CHECKLIST

FRAMING LABOR

Pre-Work Inspection: (to be completed prior to beginning work)
Date Completed _____

___ Contractor has building plans.

___ Quantity of materials list has been received.

___ Work area is clean and free of debris.

___ Foundation is complete, square, plumb, and anchor bolts are in place.

___ All formboards have been removed from foundation.

___ Material is on site and ready to be used.

___ Access for crane is adequate, as needed.

___ Trusses are on site and ready to install.

___ Temporary electrical power is available.

Final Inspection: (to be completed before Trade Contractor leaves jobsite)   Date Completed _____

___ Sill sealer insulation has been installed at all exterior walls and walls separating house from garage. Sill sealer extends slightly on each side of bottom plates. It is visible for all inspections.

___ All bottom plates are 2x4 (minimum) pressure-treated wood. Only pressure-treated material is in contact with concrete.

___ All anchor bolts have washers and nuts.

___ All exterior walls are constructed of 2x4 studs set 16 inches on center.

___ Interior nonload-bearing walls are constructed of 2x4 studs set 24 inches on center (minimum).

___ Interior load-bearing walls are constructed of 2x4 studs set 16 inches on center.

___ If the plans call for 2x6 studs in interior load-bearing walls they are set 16 inches on center.

___ Basement load-bearing walls are 2x6 studs set 16 inches on center.

___ All top plates are doubled 2x4 utility-grade material.

___ All headers have a wood grade stamp visible.

___ Laminated beams are in place and secure for individual double garage doors. Grade stamp is visible.

___ Headers resting securely on trimmers/jacks, are installed for individual double garage doors.

___ Brick lintel rests securely on and overlaps outside of jacks over garage doors, as needed.

___ All window and door openings are level, plumb, and square, and built to the correct size. All windows and doors have been checked using a level and framing square.

___ All bifold doors over carpet with jambs and casing are 82 inches high and 2 inches wider than the doors or framed per the manufacturer's rough opening specifications.

___ All bifold doors over vinyl with jambs and casings are 81 inches high and 2 inches wider than the doors or framed per the manufacturer's rough opening specifications.

___ Bifold doors with drywall jambs over vinyl are 80-1/2 inches high and 1-1/4 inches wider than the doors or framed per the manufacturer's rough opening specifications.

___ Bifold doors with drywall jambs over carpet are 81-1/2 inches high and 1-1/2 inches wider than the doors or framed per the manufacturer's rough opening specifications.

___ Exterior and interior doors over carpet are 83 inches high and 2 inches wider than the door or framed per the manufacturer's rough opening specifications.

___ Exterior and interior doors over vinyl are 82 inches high and 2 inches wider than the door or framed per the manufacturer's rough opening specifications.

___ All windows are framed 1-1/2 inches wider and higher than the window size or framed per the manufacturer's rough opening specifications.

___ Sliding doors are framed 82 inches high and 1-1/2 inches wider than the door or framed per the manufacturer's rough opening specifications.

___ All cuts are square. Anything less than 3/8 inch is shimmed. Anything more than 3/8 inch is replaced.

___ Trusses are set as per layout from truss manufacturer.

___ All joist hangers are installed and nailed. There are no empty holes.

___ **No truss is cut, notched, nicked, or otherwise damaged.**

___ Roof is level within 1/8 inch in 8 feet.
___ All exterior corner walls are braced using metal lateral bracing.
___ All pony walls are secure with no give, sway, or movement.
___ All subflooring is glued and screwed.
___ Subfloor does not give, creak, or squeak due to loose, or improperly installed subflooring.
___ No areas of the subfloor float at joints and there are no squeaks.
___ All subflooring is installed with a 1/8-inch gap between pieces.
___ All subflooring fits within 1/16 inch of all walls.
___ Subfloor is level 1/8 inch in 8 feet.
___ Any subfloors with gaps larger than 1/8 of an inch are filled with durock compound, then smoothed and sanded.
___ Any place with subflooring pieces overlap has been planed, smoothed, and leveled.
___ Hallway walls are plumb and level.
___ Walls at cabinet locations are plumb, level and square (Kitchen, bath, hallway, office, laundry, etc).
___ Columns are plumb, level and square.
___ Temporary stairs are set at each level.
___ Temporary handrails are installed on all stairs.
___ Safety bracing is installed around all openings with drops of more than 2 feet. Such openings are blocked with an "X" with a crossbar running horizontally across the opening.
___ Garden tub and tub/shower units are in set inside bathroom areas.
___ All nails are firmly set. No bent nails are protruding into any area that will receive door casings, drywall, or other types of finishes.
___ No studs are warped.
___ All fire blocking and draft stops are installed per code (chimney chases, HVAC duct chases, stair runs, floor joists, under tubs, around showers, etc.).
___ Extra blocking is installed at shower stalls, windows, doors, corners, and other areas.
___ Decking is installed with plyclips set 24 inches on center.
___ Decking is level to 1/2 inch in 2 feet.

___ Decking is securely attached to supports in order to receive roofing nails and fasteners.

___ All holes are cut, per plans, for all roof vents.

___ Exterior sheathing is installed according to manufacturer's instructions. There are no broken pieces of sheathing, and no gaps or missing pieces.

___ Wind bracing is installed at gable ends (see truss manufacturer's calculations/layout).

___ Scuttle holes or disappearing stairs are framed according to plans.

___ If framer is required to set windows, all windows are set level, plumb, and square. All windows operate correctly and lock smoothly.

___ If framer is required to set exterior doors, all doors are square, plumb, shimmed, and the required special bolts furnished by the manufacturer are installed per manufacturer's instructions in each door.

___ Deadwood is installed throughout house.

___ Door thresholds are braced with pressure-treated wood.

___ All temporary bracing, except safety bracing, has been removed.

___ All brick lentils are installed as required and reach outside edge of supporting jacks/trimmers.

___ Preliminary insulation has been installed behind tub/showers on exterior walls, exterior channels, etc.

___ All roof sheathing is installed with a 1/8-inch gap between pieces.

___ From interior of house, all fasteners in roof sheathing are in framing members. Any areas where fasteners have missed framing members and are exposed, must be removed and refastened. Especially under eves – Contractor shall remove all exposed nails!

___ All trash and building debris has been removed from house and site to correct area.

___ House has been broom-swept.

___ Excess material is in garage.

___ Excess materials have been counted and noted on quantity list.

QUALITY INSPECTION CHECKLIST

GARAGE DOORS

Pre-Work Inspection: (to be completed prior to beginning work)
Date Completed _____

___ Specifications, Colors, Plans, etc. have been reviewed with Contractor.
___ Garage door opening(s) is framed and the dimensions verified as correct.
___ Headers/lintels, etc., are installed level, plumb, and square.
___ Garage is clean, broom-swept, and free of debris.

Final Inspection: (to be completed before Trade Contractor leaves jobsite)   Date Completed _____

___ Garage door(s) is installed using correct number, size, type, color, etc.
___ Door(s) operates smoothly.
___ Door lock(s) operates smoothly and correctly.
___ Weathersealer/weatherstripping is installed.
___ Spring tension is adjusted properly, as required.
___ Door(s) is level, plumb, square, and scribed to existing garage floor.
___ Door(s) is undamaged.
___ Door opener(s) operate correctly. Openers are hung in accordance with manufacturer's specifications. One opener per door has been received.
___ Remote openers operate correctly.
___ Door sensors are installed and are operational.
___ Garage is clean, broom-swept, and free of debris.
___ Construction debris has been removed to designated location.

QUALITY INSPECTION CHECKLIST

GUTTERING

Pre-Work Inspection: (to be completed prior to beginning work)
Date Completed _____

___ Plans have been reviewed, the house walked, and any special areas noted.

___ Outside area of house is clean and free of construction debris.

___ Siding/Stucco is complete. All trim is installed and undamaged.

___ Roofing is complete.

___ Final grading is complete.

___ Windows are intact and none are broken.

___ If yard is landscaped, landscape is undamaged.

Final Inspection: (to be completed before Trade Contractor leaves jobsite)   Date Completed _____

___ Windows are intact and none are broken.

___ Trim and siding are undamaged.

___ Landscape is undamaged.

___ Gutters are firmly attached to house.

___ Gutters and downspouts contain only minor piecing.

___ Gutters have no holes or gaps.

___ Gutters have positive fall towards downspouts.

___ An adequate number of downspouts are installed.

___ Downspouts are firmly attached to house with no gaps or bows.

___ Downspouts terminate no more than 6 inches from grade and flow correctly.

___ Downspouts continue through deck if necessary.

___ Downspout hole through deck is cut smoothly and to the correct size.

___ Splashblocks are in place in valleys.

QUALITY INSPECTION CHECKLIST

HEATING and AIR CONDITIONING (FINAL)

Initial Inspection: (to be completed prior to beginning work)
Date Completed _____

___ Drywall is complete with no damage.

___ Painting is complete with no damage.

___ Trim is complete with no damage.

___ Windows are intact and unbroken.

___ There is no damage to vinyl, cabinets, etc.

___ Inside of HVAC boots/cans have been painted black.

___ House is clean and free of debris.

Final Inspection: (to be completed before Trade Contractor leaves jobsite)   Date Completed _____

___ Coverings are removed from ductwork.

___ Grills are installed square and level. In vinyl areas grills are flush to floor and do not tilt more than 1/4 inch when stepped on.

___ All grills in ceilings are fitted flush with ceiling and have proper sealing material.

___ All other grills fit snugly.

___ HVAC units have been tested to verify correct airflow.

___ Thermostats are square and level.

___ Thermostats have been tested.

___ Instruction and warranty manuals for thermostats, air conditioner, and heater have been placed in kitchen drawer to left of range.

___ Air conditioning condensation unit is set level and operating.

___ Condensation pump, if applicable, is clean, free of debris, and operating properly.

___ For attic unit, condensation pan and drain pipe are free of any obstructions.

___ Hot water tank vent pipe is installed.

___ Correct FAU and Condenser unit size are installed per plan

___ Electrical wiring is appropriate size for FAU and Condenser unit installed.

___ House is clean and free of debris.

___ House has passed final HVAC inspection.

QUALITY INSPECTION CHECKLIST

HEATING and AIR CONDITIONING (ROUGH)

Pre-Work Inspection: (to be completed prior to beginning work)
Date Completed _____

___ Permits have been received.

___ Necessary framing (chases, etc.) are complete.

___ Temporary stairs are in place.

___ Temporary handrails and safety bracing are in place.

___ Plumber has completed work, pipes are in place, etc.

___ Interior work area is clean and free of debris.

___ Site is clean and free of debris.

___ Electricity is available.

___ If units are to be set in attic, the scuttle hole for attic HVAC equipment access is framed, the HVAC unit area is floored, and adequate working area is available.

___ HVAC units have been verified for correct type, tonnage, and wire sizing.

Final Inspection: (to be completed before Trade Contractor leaves jobsite)   Date Completed _____

___ Heating unit(s) has been set with the necessary clearances on all sides.

___ No ductwork is crimped, bent, or damaged so as to restrict airflow.

___ Adequate space in heating unit area has been verified so that ductwork will not obstruct necessary maintenance, changing of filters, etc.

___ Attic unit is properly set, and ducts are not crimped, bent, or otherwise damaged if units are to be placed in attic.

___ All piping to the exterior of the house is complete and sealed properly.

___ All ducts are properly secured to boots/cans.

___ All ducts are properly sealed at the heat exchanger.

___ All ductwork is properly secured.

___ All air returns and vents are properly sealed and placed per plan.

___ All ducts are securely covered.

___ All gas cutoffs/shut offs are installed properly and are accessible (fireplace, clothes dryer, and furnace).

___ Locations of thermostats are correct per plan.

___ Gas pressure is adequate.

___ System has passed rough HVAC inspection.

___ House is broom-swept and clear of debris.

___ No debris is left on lot.

QUALITY INSPECTION CHECKLIST

INSULATION

Pre-Work Inspection: (to be completed prior to beginning work) Date Completed _____

___ Plans have been reviewed, including finished basement.

___ Purchase order has been received or picked up.

___ Rough inspections are completed and the house has passed inspections.

___ House is clean and free of debris.

___ All windows are intact and unbroken.

___ Exterior doors are weatherstripped and sealed.

___ All windows are weatherstripped and sealed.

___ Bottom plate is sill sealed.

___ Top plates and headers are poly sealed.

___ Temporary stairs, if required, are in place.

___ Temporary handrails and safety bracing are in place.

___ HVAC ductwork is installed.

___ Ducts are covered and protected.

___ Plumbing pipes, tubs, showers, etc., are installed and undamaged.

___ Electrical wiring and boxes are in place.

___ Exterior insulation and sheathing board are still in place, unbroken, undamaged, or repaired with no gaps or missing pieces.

___ All penetrations to the outside are sealed.

Final Inspection: (to be completed before Trade Contractor leaves jobsite)   Date Completed _____

___ All windows are intact.

___ Tubs, showers, etc., are undamaged.

___ All temporary handrails and safety bracing are intact.

___ A minimum of three (3) rulers are clearly visible in the attic and are in contact with the ceiling decking.

___ All wall batts fit snugly at the top, bottom, and sides, and are fastened correctly and cover all areas.

___ Insulation is not doubled over or compressed.

___ Vaults and/or tray ceilings have batt insulation.

___ Moisture barrier/Vapor retarder is installed, if required.

___ Insulation is of the correct R-value in all areas for climate zone.

___ Attic access hatch/door is insulated.

___ Basement walls are insulated including the block foundation if the basement is finished.

___ Ceilings of garages and/or basements that are under heated areas are insulated.

___ Walls between unheated areas and heated areas are insulated.

___ All attic access areas are weather-stripped.

___ Insulation is not stuffed behind, or in front of wiring or plumbing. Insulation should be split, and should wrap (or sandwich) wiring/plumbing.

___ In cold climates water pipes shall have at least two thirds of

the insulation between the water pipe and the outside. If the pipe is near the outside, as much insulation as possible (without compressing the insulation) shall be placed behind the pipe and no insulation shall be placed between the pipe and the inside.

___ Insulation is cut around receptacle boxes and is not stuffed behind or blocking the front of the box.

___ All windows and exterior doors have insulation in jacks(trimmers) and headers. **DO NOT USE EXPANDING FOAM AROUND VINYL FRAMED WINDOWS, UNLESS RECOMMENDED BY MANUFACTURER.**

___ Required ventilation must be maintained: for eaves or soffit vents, one-inch (1") of unblocked free air space between the roof sheathing and the insulation is required.

___ Insulation shall cover all IC rated lighting fixtures.

___ Fixtures that are not IC rated (e.g., halogen lamps, heat lamps) need to be enclosed in an airtight box that meets fire codes, and the box covered with insulation. If fixtures are not IC rated and not enclosed in such a box, they should be replaced or boxed before insulation is completed.

___ Correct size of batt insulation is placed under HVAC platforms, walks, and other areas in attic that will be unable to receive blown-in insulation.

___ House is clean and broom-swept.

___ All building debris has been removed to dumpster.

QUALITY INSPECTION CHECKLIST

LANDSCAPING

Pre-Work Inspection: (to be completed prior to beginning work)
Date Completed _____

___ Plans have been reviewed with Contractor and the lot walked.

___ Yard area is clean and free of debris.

___ Swales and berms are established.

___ All lines, pipes, etc., are buried.

___ Temporary power pole is removed.

___ Drive and walks are undamaged.

Final Inspection: (to be completed before Trade Contractor leaves jobsite)   Date Completed _____

___ Formboards are removed and stacked in garage.

___ Drives and walks are undamaged.

___ Swales and berms are finalized.

___ Fall is 6 inches of fall within 10 feet of house.

___ There is a minimum of 8 inches between bottom of siding and final grade in all areas.

___ Water flow and direction are correct.

___ There are no low areas that will permit the pooling of water.

___ Yard has a level, attractive appearance.

___ There are no obvious hills, gullies, washes, low spots, or bulges in yard areas.

___ Sod, if required, is healthy, with no gaps. Sod is stapled and rolled.

___ Yard is seeded. Seed can be seen clearly when straw is moved out of way.

___ Fertilizer has been applied. Fertilizer can be seen when straw is moved out of way.

___ Sod and seed have been watered.

___ Planter areas are neatly edged and appropriate ground cover applied.

___ Trees and shrubs are firmly planted, healthy looking, and watered.

___ Areas not requiring grass have had appropriate ground cover applied and are neat in appearance.

___ Yard is clean and free of trash and debris.

QUALITY INSPECTION CHECKLIST

MIRRORS

Pre-Work Inspection: (to be completed prior to beginning work)
Date Completed _____

___ Contractor has specifications for mirrors, has ordered mirrors, and has an expected delivery date.

___ Drywall and painting are complete, and have had sufficient time to dry. Never install mirrors on unsealed/unpainted wall.

___ Cabinets are installed.

___ Drywall and paint are undamaged.

___ Counter tops are installed, undamaged, and protected.

___ Windows are installed and undamaged.

___ House is clean, broom-swept, and free of debris.

Final Inspection: (to be completed before Trade Contractor leaves jobsite)   Date Completed _____

___ All windows are intact and unbroken.

___ Drywall and paint are undamaged.

___ Countertops are undamaged and remain protected.

___ Mirror installers wear gloves to prevent damage from skin-borne salts or chemicals from coming into contact with mirror backing.

___ Mirror is installed at least 3/8" above closest surface to bottom of mirror. Never install mirror in contact with counter top/back splash.

___ Mirrors are installed level, plumb, and square by 1/8" per 6 feet.

___ Mirrors are installed into solid backing, per plan and per specification.

___ J-Channel has weep holes (if used).

___ Mirror has 3mm neoprene setting pads between the mirror and clip/channel.

___ Mirrors are undamaged with no visible imperfections, peeling, flaking, chips, cracks, scratches, discoloration, or damage to backing under normal lighting conditions from a 3 foot distance.

___ Adhesives (if used) should be a "neutral-cure" product. Avoid adhesives with solvents like acetone, toluene, methylene chloride, acetic acid, etc.

___ Mirrors are installed per manufacturer's recommendations.

___ House is clean and broom-swept, and debris has been removed.

QUALITY INSPECTION CHECKLIST

PAINTING (FINAL)

Pre-Work Inspection: (to be completed prior to beginning work)
Date Completed _____

___ There is no damage to tubs, showers, countertops, stairs, cabinets, windows, flooring, etc.

___ All protective coverings are in place (tubs, countertops, flooring, etc.).

___ All drywall repairs have been completed, surface is smooth and sanded with no raised facepaper from over-sanding.

___ Wall texture is consistent throughout.

___ All damaged trim has been repaired or replaced.

___ There is no carpet on the floor.

___ House is ready to be painted.

___ House is clean, broom-swept, and free of debris.

Final Inspection: (to be completed before Trade Contractor leaves jobsite)   Date Completed _____

___ Second coat of paint applied to walls is smooth, with no runs, drips, lumps, color variations, streaking, or light spots.

___ Second coat of trim paint applied to trim and doors is smooth, with no runs, drips, lumps, color variations, streaking, or light spots.

___ All stairs and handrails are stained or painted per plan.

___ All stained areas have a uniform appearance and complete coverage.

___ Varnish is applied smoothly and uniformly to all stained areas.

___ There is no damage to drywall, stairs, handrails, trim, etc.

___ Paint spills have been **removed without damage** to vinyl, wood floors, tubs, showers, countertops, etc.

___ Paint has been removed from window glass and frames.

___ Paint has been removed from door hinges and all hardware.

___ Doors have been rehung, and are square, level, plumb, and back where they belong.

___ Thresholds are painted/stained at all exterior doors.

___ No defects are visible under sunlight and normal house lighting from a distance of 6 feet for the entire interior paint job.

___ There is no paint residue in sinks.

___ Interior walls are smooth with no drips, runs, lumps, bumps, color variations, or streaking.

___ Interior walls have uniform coverage after first coat is sprayed.

___ All rough spots have been repaired in interior trim. Nail holes are filled and sanded smooth.

___ First coat trim paint applied.

___ Inside of HVAC cans/boots are painted black.

___ Six sides of each door has been painted (including top and bottom).

___ Excess trim paint on walls has been cleaned off.

___ Over-spray has been cleaned from windows (glass and frames).

___ Paint buckets, sprayers, etc. are not set on top of finished surfaces, ie. Countertops, flooring, tubs, garage floors, drive, patio, deck, etc.

___ There is no damage to finished surfaces from spills, drips, etc.

___ There is no damage to cabinets or countertops.

___ All interior wood is caulked.

___ Tubs, sinks, showers, flooring, etc., have no damage.

___ Empty paint buckets are removed from site.

___ Paint brushes, sprayers, buckets, etc. do not get washed out in sinks, gutters, landscape, etc.

___ No debris in garages.

___ Debris has been removed to the dumpster.

___ House is clean and broom-swept.

QUALITY INSPECTION CHECKLIST

PAINTING (ROUGH)

Pre-Work Inspection: (to be completed prior to beginning work)
Date Completed _____

___ Plans, specifications, and colors have been reviewed with Contractor.

___ Windows are intact with none broken.

___ Flooring is protected.

___ Tubs, showers, countertops, etc., are protected.

___ All drywall is installed, taped, mudded, and sanded.

___ Texture is complete and consistent throughout.

___ Drywall is straight with no bows or depressions.

___ Joints in drywall are smooth and clean.

___ Drywall has no excessive nicks, gouges, scrapes, etc.

___ Drywall has no raised face-paper from over-sanding.

___ Corners have no hairline cracks.

___ Drywall has no nail pops or loose nails.

___ Trim fits properly around all windows and doors

___ Paint grade window and door casing, crown molding, chair rail, have been caulked and nail holes are filled and sanded.

___ Baseboard has no nicks, gouges, scratches, damage, etc.

___ Nails are set properly in baseboard at correct depth with no protruding nails.

___ Baseboard is secured tightly, corners are correct and tight.

___ Baseboard around cabinets is tacked in place.

___ All doors are installed according to plan, and are plumb, square, the proper distance for carpet or vinyl, and swing correctly.

___ All bifold doors are square, plumb, and tracks are installed tightly.

___ Attic accesses are installed correctly and all trim is in place.

___ There is no missing trim in any room.

___ Chair rail or crown is installed, if required by plan or options.

___ House is broom-swept, clean, and free of debris.

Final Inspection: (to be completed before Trade Contractor leaves jobsite)   Date Completed _____

___ Exterior wall paint has uniform coverage, and no light spots.

___ Exterior trim paint has uniform coverage, uniform color, and no paint of walls.

___ Exterior metal painted uniform color and no paint on walls/roof tile

___ Exterior paint job inspected from 6-foot distance (entire job) with no visible defects.

___ No paint is on windows, brick, stucco, doors, concrete flatwork, or other areas.

___ Metal lintels are clean (no rust) and painted black with rust-proof paint.

___ All exterior wood is caulked.

___ All gaps between the brickmold and brick are caulked.

___ All thresholds are caulked.

___ Windows are intact with none broken.

___ Paint is stored properly.

___ MSDS sheets displayed.

___ No debris in garages.

___ Empty paint buckets are picked up and removed from jobsite.

QUALITY INSPECTION CHECKLIST

PAINTING (TOUCH-UP)

Pre-Work Inspection: (to be completed prior to beginning work)
Date Completed _____

___ All work by other trade contractors is complete, except the cleaning crew.

Final Inspection: (to be completed before Trade Contractor leaves jobsite)   Date Completed _____

___ All areas of paint have been inspected and no missed repairs were found.

___ Touch-up paint areas blend with surrounding areas (no difference visible from 6 feet in sunlight from windows and under normal house lighting).

___ No excess paint is on any area (windows, trim, doors, floors, etc.).

___ Correct colors & sheens were used. i.e. Flat pain is not used to touch up in areas painted with semi-gloss paint, etc.

___ House is clean and free of debris, and ready for the cleaning crew.

QUALITY INSPECTION CHECKLIST

PLUMBING (FINAL)

Pre-Work Inspection: (to be completed prior to beginning work)
Date Completed _____

___ House is clean and free of debris from prior trade contractors.

___ Windows are intact and unbroken.

___ Flooring in water closets are installed and undamaged.

___ Tub(s) is undamaged.

___ Cabinets are installed.

___ Gas test has been completed (after cabinets have been installed).

___ Correct dimensions for water closets (walls, cabinets, etc.) are verified.

___ All safety bracing, temporary handrails, etc., are in place, if required.

Final Inspection: (to be completed before Trade Contractor leaves jobsite)   Date Completed _____

___ All fixtures are set, and are not tarnished, chipped, or otherwise defective.

___ All fixtures and faucets (brand and type) correspond to plans and specifications.

___ All fixtures have been tested for operation.

___ Garbage disposal operates smoothly.

___ Dishwasher operates evenly, with no leaks. Run through entire cycle.

___ There are no scratches, dents, or chipped surfaces on appliances.

___ No leaks have been found.

___ Toilets are placed, level, and caulked after finished floor is installed.

___ Toilets are operational, adjusted correctly and do not continuously run, or seep.

___ Test all fixtures for filling and draining. Drains shall flow freely.

___ Turn on all sink faucets and flush all toilets at the same time to see if they'll all work without a major reduction in water flow.

___ Turn on faucets, tubs, and drains on upper floors. See if any stains from on downstairs ceiling beneath those fixtures.

___ No excessive noise is heard from water pipes.

___ No water hammering when shutting off water.

___ No surface defects in faucets, tubs or showers have been found.

___ Tub(s) and shower(s) are fully secured to wall.

___ Showerhead pipes, tub spouts, etc. should be secured and should not move in or out.

___ If pedestal sink, water shutoff valves are accessible and usable.

___ All faucets and showerheads are in alignment (level and straight).

___ Regular water shutoffs are all accessible and in working order.

___ Correct number of water shutoffs have been verified.

___ Turn on all outdoor spigots. Make sure they close easily and completely.

___ Water shutoff at street works correctly.

___ Water meter box is installed level, and is not located in drainage swale.

___ Hot and cold water are identified at each shutoff valve (including clothes washer shutoff).

___ Hot water is on the left, cold on the right.

___ Correct number of outside faucets have been verified and all are working.

___ Strainer and stopper are in good condition and placed in drawer in kitchen.

___ Emergency key for garbage disposal is in drawer in kitchen with strainer and stopper.

___ Warranty and instruction manuals for hot water heater and garbage disposal are in kitchen drawer to left of range.

___ Hot water heater works (checked at each faucet) and is installed per manufacturer's instructions.

___ Water heater tank has a TPRV (Temperature Pressure Relief Valve) discharge pipe installed.

___ Test the TPRV to see if it opens easily and seals shut when closed.

___ Water heater drain pan and discharge pipe installed, if required.

___ Water heater's manufacturers identification label in on water heater. Should identify manufacturer, model number, serial number, date manufactured, etc.

___ Anti-siphon valves, vacuum relief valves/vacuum breakers, backflow preventers, etc. are installed as required.
___ All inspections have been passed.
___ House and site are clean, broom-swept, and free of debris.

QUALITY INSPECTION CHECKLIST

PLUMBING (ROUGH)

Pre-Work Inspection: (to be completed prior to beginning work)
Date Completed _____

___ Framing items for plumbing are complete.

___ Temporary stairs, handrails, and safety bracing are in place, as required.

___ Tubs are placed in bathroom areas, and protected from damage.

___ Deadwood/backing has been installed behind shower stall for door installation.

___ Blocking or deadwood has been installed as required i.e. towel bars, toilet paper holder, etc.

___ House is clean, broom-swept, and free of prior Trade Contractor's debris.

Final Inspection: (to be completed before Trade Contractor leaves jobsite)   Date Completed _____

___ Tubs, showers, etc., are set.

___ All water supply piping is installed.

___ Drains and vents are installed.

___ Waste vents should exit through the roof on the back side of the house if possible.

___ No solder or flux is on floor areas.

___ All safety bracing, temporary handrails, etc., are still in place.

___ Rough plumbing inspection has been passed.

___ Pipes are secured in walls, not hanging freely, etc.

___ Coil overflow pans in attic are connected to PVC drains and have positive fall.

___ Condensate drains are installed, as required.

___ House is broom-swept, clean and free of debris.

QUALITY INSPECTION CHECKLIST

PLUMBING (UNDERGROUND)

Pre-Work Inspection: (to be completed prior to beginning work)
Date Completed _____

___ Contractor has plans.

___ Work area is clean and free of debris, ready to dig underground lines.

___ Foundation/Footings are dug and formed.

___ Electricity is at site.

Final Inspection: (to be completed before Trade Contractor leaves jobsite)   Date Completed _____

___ Plumbing is set, and capped and protected as required.

QUALITY INSPECTION CHECKLIST

POURED WALL FOUNDATIONS

Pre-Work Inspection: (to be completed prior to beginning work)
Date Completed _____

___ Contractor has plans.

___ Work area is clean and free of debris.

___ Footing(s) is poured, and alignment, square corners, etc., are verified.

___ Dimensions are correct.

___ Stakes are set and locations are correct.

___ Straightness (alignment) of lines has been verified.

___ All setbacks, bay windows, fireplace(s), porches, stoops, etc., are clearly marked and dimensions have been checked.

___ All materials are on site and ready to be used.

___ Area is clear and a stable base is available for concrete trucks.

Final Inspection: (to be completed before Trade Contractor leaves jobsite)   Date Completed _____

___ All walls are true, plumb, and square.

___ There are no cracks.

___ Foundation variance does not exceed 1/2 inch out of level in 20 feet, with no ridges or depressions in excess of 1/4 inch within any 32-inch measurement.

___ Foundation walls are not more than 1 inch out of level over the entire surface and do not vary more than 1/2 inch out of square when measured along the diagonal of a 6x8x10-foot triangle at any corner.

___ All line and pinholes are filled.

___ There are no honeycombs.

___ Ties are broken off and all tie holes filled.

___ Seams between the foundation and footing are sealed watertight.

___ Trench(es) is free and clear of all debris.

___ Anchor bolts are 6 feet on center and not more than 12 inches from corners, unless otherwise noted on plans.

___ All excess material is stacked and protected from weather.

___ Jobsite area is clean and free of debris, and excess concrete has been removed to driveway.

___ All formboards have been removed and stacked with excess material.

___ Field measurements match measurements on Contractor's invoice.

___ Batch tickets have been collected from concrete truck driver.

QUALITY INSPECTION CHECKLIST

ROOFING LABOR

Pre- Work Inspection: (to be completed prior to beginning work)
Date Completed _____

___ Work area is clean and free of debris.

___ All material is on site, matches specifications, style, color, and is ready to be used.

___ Decking is complete, dry, and there are no warped deck boards.

___ Windows have not been installed.

___ Trade Contractor has OSHA-approved equipment on site, with no toe boards.

Final Inspection: (to be completed before Trade Contractor leaves jobsite)   Date Completed _____

___ Roof is complete.

___ Materials are straight and true.

___ Materials are secure with none loose or broken.

___ Ridge vents (or turtle-back vents) are installed per plan, as required.

___ Ridges are covered.

___ Drip edge is correct.

___ All valleys are completed and covered with shingles.

___ All nail holes are sealed.

___ All roof vents are installed per plan ie. Dormer vents, etc..

___ All excess material is stacked in one area, counted, and verified.

___ Jobsite is clean. All trash, debris, and shingle scraps have been removed.

QUALITY INSPECTION CHECKLIST

SHELVING

Pre-Work Inspection: (to be completed prior to beginning work)
Date Completed _____

___ Drywall and painting are complete and ready for shelving.

___ Drywall and paint are undamaged.

___ Windows are installed and undamaged.

___ House is clean, broom-swept, and free of debris.

Final Inspection: (to be completed before Trade Contractor leaves jobsite)   Date Completed _____

___ All windows are intact and unbroken.

___ Drywall and paint is undamaged.

___ Shelving is installed level, plumb, square, and secure.

___ Shelving is installed per plan.

___ House is clean and broom-swept.

___ Debris has been removed to correct area.

QUALITY INSPECTION CHECKLIST

SHOWER DOORS

Pre-Work Inspection: (to be completed prior to beginning work)
Date Completed _____

___ Plans, specifications, and colors have been verified.

___ Shower is installed and ready for shower doors.

___ Windows are installed and undamaged.

___ House is clean, broom-swept, and free of debris.

Final Inspection: (to be completed before Trade Contractor leaves jobsite)   Date Completed _____

___ All windows are intact and unbroken.

___ Shower stall is undamaged.

___ Shower doors are installed level, plumb, square, and operate smoothly.

___ Shower doors are installed per plan.

___ House is clean and broom-swept.

___ Debris has been removed to correct area.

QUALITY INSPECTION CHECKLIST

SHUTTERS

Pre-Work Inspection: (to be completed prior to beginning work)
Date Completed _____

___ Shutters are correct type, size, material, and color.

___ Siding, brick, stucco, etc., are complete.

___ Windows are installed and undamaged.

___ Shutters have been painted.

Final Inspection: (to be completed before Trade Contractor leaves jobsite)   Date Completed _____

___ All windows are intact and unbroken.

___ Siding, brick, and stucco are undamaged.

___ Shutters are installed level, plumb, and square with no bows or bends.

___ Shutters are undamaged.

___ If landscaping is installed, there has been no damage to landscaping.

QUALITY INSPECTION CHECKLIST

SIDING AND CORNICE LABOR

Pre-Work Inspection: (to be completed prior to beginning work)
Date Completed _____

___ Plans have been reviewed with Contractor.

___ Materials are on site and ready to be used.

___ Area around house is free and clear of debris.

___ All insulated boards are installed with no open areas or gaps and no broken boards.

___ Insulation boards are dry.

___ Roof is completed.

___ Windows and doors are set.

___ Windows are intact and unbroken.

Final Inspection: (to be completed before Trade Contractor leaves jobsite)   Date Completed _____

___ From interior of house all fasteners are in framing members. Any area where fasteners have missed framing members and are protruding through insulation boards must be refastened.

___ All broken insulation and siding boards have been repaired and sealed.

___ Siding is installed per manufacturer's installation instructions.

___ Siding is level and straight with no more than a 1/4-inch deviation in 10 feet.

___ Exterior trim is level, plumb, and undamaged.

___ Exterior trim is not split or broken, and does not have large knots or holes.

___ Exterior trim is secured tightly to framing members.

___ Gaps in exterior trim do not exceed 1/4 inch and have been caulked.

___ Facia, rake boards, soffits, and soffit areas are all complete. Material is undamaged with no holes, splits, broken boards, large knots, etc.

___ All holes, nicks, gouges, etc., are caulked and/or repaired.

___ Site is clean and free of debris and excess material is stacked at front of lot.

QUALITY INSPECTION CHECKLIST

SLABS

Pre-Work Inspection: (to be completed prior to beginning work)
Date Completed _____

___ Contractor has building plans.
___ Work area is clean and free of debris.
___ Foundation is complete, aligned and corners are square.
___ Seam between foundation and footing is sealed watertight.
___ Dimensions are correct.
___ Straightness (alignment) of lines have been verified.
___ All materials are on site and ready to be used.
___ There should be no presence of ground water, mud, or soft spots where concrete is being poured
___ Temperature is above 40°F.
___ Clear access and a stable base is available for concrete trucks.

Final Inspection: (to be completed before Trade Contractor leaves jobsite)   Date Completed _____

___ Slab is level and plumb with no pits, depressions, or areas of unevenness exceeding 1/4 inch in 32 inches.
___ Slab surface is trowel-finished and smooth.
___ Garage floor is poured and broom-finished.
___ Garage floor slopes toward door per code with no pits, depressions, or areas of unevenness exceeding 1/4 inch in 32 inches.
___ Patio, stoop, and porch are poured and broom-finished with correct slope for drainage.
___ Patio, stoop, and porch are no more than 1-1/2 inches from the house slab.
___ Expansion joints should be installed between driveway and sidewalk; foundation and driveway; garage and driveway; patio, stoop, porch and foundation, etc. Joints should be 1/2-inch wide and level with the top of the concrete surface.

___ Control joints are used/installed.
___ No exposed aggregate is in any area.
___ No cracks or displacement are in any area.
___ Excess sand/stone is spread in driveway cut.
___ Excess concrete runoff has been moved to driveway cut.
___ Jobsite is clean and free of debris.
___ Foundation trench is free and clear of debris.
___ Foundation is clean of any concrete spills, overruns, etc.
___ Batch tickets have been collected from concrete truck driver.

QUALITY INSPECTION CHECKLIST

STAIRS (PREBUILT)

Pre-Work Inspection: (to be completed prior to beginning work)
Date Completed _____

___ Plans have been reviewed with Contractor.

___ House has been field-measured.

___ Work area is clear of debris.

Final Inspection: (to be completed before Subcontractor leaves jobsite)
Date Completed _____

___ Stairs are installed in levels that require stairs.

___ Fire blocking/fire stops are installed as needed.

___ All sets of stairs fit correctly.

___ All sets of stairs are the correct type.

___ Heights and runs have been measured and are correct for all sets of stairs.

___ All sets of stairs do not creak, squeak, or move.

___ Bracing has been checked (nailed and glued) and verified for all sets of stairs.

___ No patching has been made to any stairs due to incorrect measurements.

___ Temporary stairs have been moved to garage.

___ All risers are protected on all sets of stairs.

___ All finished wood surface has double protection. No finished wood surface is visible.

___ If extra stairs are required for the garage they are the correct height and are correctly installed.

___ No wood is in direct contact with concrete unless wood is pressure treated.

QUALITY INSPECTION CHECKLIST

TRIM LABOR

Pre-Work Inspection: (to be completed prior to beginning work)
Date Completed _____

___ Material is on site and ready to be used.

___ House is clean, broom-swept, and free of debris.

___ Garage is clean.

___ Windows are intact and unbroken.

___ Stairs are installed.

___ Drywall is undamaged.

___ Vinyl is undamaged.

___ Ducts are covered.

___ Tubs are covered and undamaged.

___ Sinks, cabinets, and countertops are covered and undamaged.

___ Cabinets are set.

___ Doors are framed plumb and of correct size. Plan used to check carpet and vinyl areas.

___ Swing of doors is clearly marked on inside of each doorjamb.

___ Disappearing stairs are installed, if required.

___ Attic access is framed.

Final Inspection: (to be completed before Trade Contractor leaves job site)   Date Completed _____

___ Windows are intact and unbroken.

___ Drywall is undamaged.

___ Vinyl is undamaged.

___ Ducts are covered.

___ Tubs are covered and undamaged.

___ Sinks, cabinets, and countertops are covered and undamaged.

___ Base molding is installed securely to walls.

___ Base molding is undamaged and all nicks, gouges, etc., are repaired and sanded.

___ Base molding is level and straight, especially in tight and/or short runs.

___ Crown if required, is secure, level, and straight.

___ Chair rails, if required, are secure, level, and straight.

___ Nail holes are correct depth with no splintering or cracking.

___ Corners are cut correctly and fit snugly.

___ Doors are hung level, plumb, and shimmed.

___ Door/Window casing is secure, level, and straight.

___ Handrails are installed to the correct length, and are straight and secure.

___ Pickets and newels are installed correctly and securely with no movement.

___ Shoe molding is installed over all vinyl, securely and tightly to the base.

___ Shoe molding cuts at doors are cut 1/4 inch or less.

___ Corners of shoe molding fit snugly and are cut correctly.

___ Stair treads are undamaged.

___ Attic access areas are trimmed per plan.

___ Excess material has been removed to garage.

___ All debris has been removed to dumpster.

___ House is clean and broom-swept.

QUALITY INSPECTION CHECKLIST

TRIM LABOR (LOCK-OUT)

Pre-Work Inspection: (to be completed prior to beginning work)

Date Completed _____

___ Doors are installed

Final Inspection: (to be completed before Trade Contractor leaves job site)   Date Completed _____

___ Doors open and close smoothly.

___ Doors latch correctly.

___ Doors lock and unlock correctly.

___ Privacy locks are installed on all bedrooms and baths.

___ Debris has been removed to dumpster.

___ House is broom-swept.

QUALITY INSPECTION CHECKLIST

WATERPROOFING

Pre-Work Inspection: (to be completed prior to beginning work)
Date Completed _____

___ Work area is clean and free of debris.

___ Foundation trench is free and clear of all debris.

___ All formboards have been removed.

___ Sides of foundation trench are sloped away from foundation to prevent cave-in.

___ No honeycombs are on poured walls.

___ No cracks are on masonry foundations or poured walls.

___ Foundation is clean and free of excess mortar, dirt, mud, etc.

Final Inspection: (to be completed before Trade Contractor leaves jobsite)   Date Completed _____

___ Waterproofing fully covers all foundation area from footing to top of grade.

___ Waterproofing is of consistent thickness with no thin or missed spots.

___ Stone is 2 inches below drain pipe and 4 inches above drain pipe, unless otherwise noted on plans.

___ Drain pipe extends a minimum of 2 feet beyond the outside edge of the footing and 6 inches above the top of the footing.

___ Work area is clear of all building debris.

___ Contractor has verified lineal footage of foundation.

___ All drain pipes are flagged to prevent damage by Trade Contractors.

QUALITY INSPECTION CHECKLIST

WINDOW and DOOR INSTALLATION

Pre-Work Inspection: (to be completed prior to beginning work)
Date Completed _____

___ Plans have been received.

___ House is clean and free of debris.

___ Framing is complete.

___ Window and door openings have been checked and dimensions are correct.

___ Electricity is available.

___ All roofing material has been on roof for at least 3 days.

Final Inspection: (to be completed before Trade Contractor leaves jobsite)   Date Completed _____

___ All windows and doors are set.

___ There are no broken windows.

___ All windows operate and lock correctly.

___ Doors swing and operate correctly.

___ Weatherstripping is installed.

___ There is no air leakage around windows or doors.

___ Do not use expanding foam around window/door frames unless approved by window/door manufacturer.

___ Window/Door sills should be supported under entire length of sill.

___ All windows are plumb, level, and square.

___ All doors are plumb, level, and square.

___ House is broom-swept, and is free and clear of debris.

ABOUT THE AUTHOR

Ryan Brautovich is an Army veteran with more than 20 years of home construction, home remodeling and building experience who has consulted for Fortune 500 home builders as well as the Top 100 privately held home building companies. He is a custom home builder in California and a California licensed general contractor. Ryan is International Code Council Certified, an International and California Building Inspector as well as an International and California Plumbing Inspector. He is a graduate of Auburn University with degrees in both Accounting and Business Management. He has consulted for the City of Lancaster (CA) Building & Safety Department, K. Hovnanian Homes, Beezer Homes, Pardee Homes, KB Homes, Standard Pacific Homes, American Premiere Homes, Richmond American Homes, DR Horton, and Frontier Homes – just to name a few.

Ryan founded the Construction H.E.L.P. Foundation, a national nonprofit organization, dedicated to advocating for and meeting the needs of individuals who have suffered at the hands of unscrupulous contractors and sub-contractors who simply took advantage of the helpless homeowner in order to make a quick buck – and either didn't finish the project, over-charged or simply took money and didn't perform the work as promised. Over the years, the number of phone calls Ryan received increased dramatically from frustrated and angry homeowners who were desperately seeking help after being ripped off by other contractors. As a result, he founded the Construction H.E.L.P. Foundation, and it's educational assistance program – Home Construction Audit – to provide assistance and education to homeowners. As the founder of the Construction H.E.L.P. Foundation, Ryan has made it the organization's daily mission to return ethics to the home building and home remodeling profession and provide homeowners with the expert help and crucial knowledge they need so that they will never be taken advantage of again.

www.ingramcontent.com/pod-product-compliance
Lightning Source LLC
Chambersburg PA
CBHW021215240426
43672CB00026B/328